I0426232

Appomattox Courthouse National Historical Park and Booker T. Washington National Monument

Weather of 2009

Natural Resource Data Series NPS/MIDN/NRDS—2010/089

Paul Knight, Tiffany Wisniewski, Chad Bahrmann, and Sonya Miller

Pennsylvania State Climate Office
503 Walker Building
Pennsylvania State University
University Park, Pennsylvania

September 2010

U.S. Department of the Interior
National Park Service
Natural Resource Program Center
Fort Collins, Colorado

The National Park Service, Natural Resource Program Center publishes a range of reports that address natural resource topics of interest and applicability to a broad audience in the National Park Service and others in natural resource management, including scientists, conservation and environmental constituencies, and the public.

The Natural Resource Data Series is intended for the timely release of basic data sets and data summaries. Care has been taken to assure accuracy of raw data values, but a thorough analysis and interpretation of the data has not been completed. Consequently, the initial analyses of data in this report are provisional and subject to change.

All manuscripts in the series receive the appropriate level of peer review to ensure that the information is scientifically credible, technically accurate, appropriately written for the intended audience, and designed and published in a professional manner. This report received informal peer review by subject-matter experts who were not directly involved in the collection, analysis, or reporting of the data. Data in this report were collected and analyzed using methods based on established, peer-reviewed protocols and were analyzed and interpreted within the guidelines of the protocols.

Views, statements, findings, conclusions, recommendations, and data in this report do not necessarily reflect views and policies of the National Park Service, U.S. Department of the Interior. Mention of trade names or commercial products does not constitute endorsement or recommendation for use by the U.S. Government.

This report is available from the Mid-Atlantic Network (http://science.nature.nps.gov/im/units/MIDN) and the Natural Resource Publications Management website (http://www.nature.nps.gov/publications/NRPM).

Please cite this publication as:

Knight, P., T. Wisniewski, C. Bahrmann, and S. Miller. 2010. Appomattox Courthouse National Historical Park and Booker T. Washington National Monument: Weather of 2009. Natural Resource Data Series NPS/MIDN/NRDS—2010/089. National Park Service, Fort Collins, Colorado.

NPS 340/105690, 404/105690, September 2010

Table of Contents

Page

Figures.. iv

Tables v

List of Key Acronyms.. vi

Introduction.. 1

Climate of the Western Piedmont Region of Virginia... 2

Observing Stations 3

Temperature Summary.. 6

Precipitation Summary... 11

Drought Status 15

References... 19

Figures

Page

Figure 1. Location of weather observing stations around Appomattox Court House National Historical Park and Booker T. Washington National Monument selected as most representative of the parks in 2009. 4

Figure 2. Maps showing departure from average monthly maximum temperature compared to the 30-year normal (1971–2000). 9

Figure 3. Maps showing departure from average monthly minimum temperature compared to the 30-year normal (1971–2000). 10

Figure 4. Maps showing percent of average monthly precipitation compared to the 30-year normal (1971–2000). 12

Figure 5. Palmer Drought Severity Index (PDSI) for the Western Piedmont, 2007–2009 16

Figure 6. Mid-month values of the Palmer Drought Severity Index for Virginia in 2009. 17

Figure 7. Mid-month values of the Palmer Drought Severity Index for the Southeast in 2009 18

Tables

Page

Table 1. List of weather observing stations around Appomattox Court House National Historical Park and Booker T. Washington National Monument selected as most representative of the parks in 2009. 5

Table 2. Status of 2009 temperature indicators compared to the 30-year normal (1971–2000) at the Lynchburg (KLYH), Roanoke (KROA) and Appomattox (APXV2) weather observing stations. 7

Table 3. Summary of 2009 monthly average temperatures for selected stations. 8

Table 4. Summary of 2009 departure from normal temperature based on 30-year normal (1971–2000) for selected stations. 8

Table 5. Seasonal temperature and precipitation rankings over 115 years for the Western Piedmont (NOAA 2010). 8

Table 6. Status of 2009 precipitation indicators compared to the 30-year normal (1971–2000) at the Lynchburg (KLYH), Roanoke (KROA), Appomattox (APXV2) and Huddleston (HUDV2) weather observing stations. 13

Table 7. Top five wettest days and top five dry spells (consecutive days with a trace or less of rainfall) during 2009 from weather observing stations at Lynchburg (KLYH), Roanoke (KROA), Blue Ridge (KMTV), Appomattox (APXV2) and Huddleston (HUDV2). 13

Table 8. Summary of 2009 monthly total precipitation for selected stations. 14

Table 9. Summary of 2009 percent of normal precipitation based on 30-year normal (1971–2000) for selected stations. 14

List of Key Acronyms

APCO   Appomattox Court House National Historical Park

BOWA   Booker T. Washington National Monument

COOP   National Weather Service Cooperative Observer Program

CWOP   Citizen Weather Observer Program

FAA   Federal Aviation Administration

IFLOWS Integrated Flood Observing and Warning System

NADP   National Atmospheric Deposition Program

NARR   North American Regional Reanalysis

NCDC   National Climatic Data Center

NHP   National Historical Park

NM   National Monument

NWS   National Weather Service

PDSI   Palmer Drought Severity Index

PRISM   Parameter-elevation Regressions on Independent Slopes Model

RAWS   Remote Automated Weather Stations

USDM   United States Drought Monitor

USGS   United States Geological Survey

Introduction

Weather and climate are widely recognized as key drivers of terrestrial and aquatic ecosystems, affecting biotic as well as abiotic ecosystem characteristics and processes. Global and regional scale climatic patterns, trends, and variations are critical to the cycling of elements, nutrients, and minerals through the ecosystems and can deliver pollutants from regional and even global sources (National Assessment Synthesis Team 2001). These variations and trends influence the fundamental properties of ecologic systems such as soil-water relationships and plant-soil processes and their disturbance rates and intensity. Information obtained from meteorological monitoring will be useful to interpreting and understanding changes in species composition, community structure, water and soil chemistry, and related landscape processes (Comiskey and Callahan 2008).

The purpose of this report is to provide a concise weather and climate summary for January 1 to December 31, 2009, and to place current patterns and trends in an appropriate historical, regional, and global context (Knight et al., in preparation). It is our intention that this report will satisfy an inherent interest in meteorological phenomena and meet the Mid-Atlantic Network (MIDN) Weather and Climate Monitoring objectives:

- Document long-term trends in weather and climate through seasonal and annual summaries of selected parameters (e.g., multiple forms of precipitation, temperature).
- Identify and document extremes and averages of climatic conditions for common parameters (e.g., precipitation, air temperature) and other parameters where sufficient data are available (e.g., wind speed and direction, solar radiation).
- Provide information on near real-time weather parameters, historical climate patterns, and climate station metadata from a single, easy-to-use Internet portal.

To accomplish these objectives, a variety of atmospheric data streams were evaluated for their quality, longevity, and applicability to the MIDN parks. Since no single weather observing network contains all the pertinent measures of atmospheric phenomena to assess ecosystem health, an objective analysis of the data networks was developed and outlined in the Weather and Climate Monitoring Protocol for the Eastern Rivers and Mountains Network and Mid-Atlantic Network of the National Park Service (Knight et al., in preparation). Through this analysis, a select number of weather/climate observing stations were chosen as representative of each park; these are the primary data sources used in the profile of 2009's climate summary and trends.

In addition to a suite of summary tables, graphs, and narratives, we specifically identify a series of key climatological indicators to report status and trends on an annual basis and periodically in separate and more thorough reports. These key indicators are further described in the protocol (Knight et al., in preparation) and summarized in this report.

Climate of the Western Piedmont Region of Virginia

Appomattox Court House National Historical Park (NHP) and Booker T. Washington National Monument (NHP) lie in Virginia Climate Division 3, known as the "Western Piedmont." A climate division is a region that is reasonably homogenous with respect to climatic and hydrologic characteristics and is frequently used for compiling climate statistics (http://www.esrl.noaa.gov/psd/data/usclimate/map.html). Virginia is divided into six climate divisions. This division is generally considered to have a humid, continental type of climate, but the varied physiographic features have a marked effect on the weather and climate of the various parts of this region. The prevailing westerly winds carry most of the weather disturbances that affect the region from the interior of the continent through the Ohio Valley, so that the Atlantic Ocean has only some influence on the climate of the area (Davey et al. 2006, Gawtry and Stenger 2007). Coastal storms do, at times, affect the day-to-day weather, especially in the winter. Infrequently, storms of tropical origin can have a significant effect, causing severe floods in some instances.

Temperatures are moderately continental with the tempering effects of the nearby mountains contributing to cloud production in the winter and mountain-valley circulation clouds reducing the heat at times during the summer. The lowest readings in the winter occur with polar air masses of Canadian origin settling over the region after a fresh snowfall. On average, Appomattox Court House NHP tends to have a greater number of sub freezing nights than Booker T. Washington NM (~92 to ~75). The highest readings of the summer happen when the sub-tropical fair weather system, the Bermuda high, pushes westward into the Carolinas; its clockwise circulation will direct hot, humid air from the Gulf region into the region. The humid southwest winds descending the crest of the Appalachians will raise the temperature several more degrees. The last freeze typically occurs in mid-April and the first frosts appear in late October.

Precipitation is fairly evenly distributed throughout the year. Annual amounts generally range between 36–52 in (914–1,321 mm), while the majority of places receive 38–44 in (965–1,118 mm). Greatest amounts usually occur in the late spring and summer months, while February is the driest month, having about 2 in (51 mm) less than the wettest months. Precipitation is somewhat greater in the mountains. During the warm season, the uneven heating over the irregular terrain leads to thunderstorms which typically form over the mountains and dissipate as they reach the Piedmont.

Surface winds blow from the west and northwest in the cold season and from the southwest during the warm half of the year. Thunderstorms follow a frequency that matches the solar cycle, occurring between the equinoxes and reaches a peak near the solstice. Hail is relatively infrequent, but flash floods and damaging thunderstorm winds affect parts of the region each summer. On average, tornadoes pass through the area about once every three years. The direct effects of an Atlantic hurricane are uncommon, though remnant rains from hurricanes and tropical storms occur most years and some have contributed to the region's worst floods. Ice storms, which can cause significant disruption, occur at irregular intervals but are primarily confined to the months between December and March (Kocin and Uccellini 2004).

Observing Stations

A total of 19 weather observing stations comprising six weather observing networks were selected around Appomattox Court House NHP and Booker T. Washington NM. Representative stations within a 100-km range of each park were chosen based on several criteria, which include proximity to the park, the representativeness of the station to the park elevation profile, the type and frequency of observations, the period of record of the data, and data availability (Knight et al., in preparation). A subset of these observing networks (IFLOWS, GOES, and CWOP; eight total stations) are not yet utilized for these reports due to limited data availability and/or lack of data quality assurance (Bureau of Land Management 1997). Moreover, the percentage of time a station reports a particular parameter (e.g., temperature) can influence data inclusion. A total of five stations were ultimately used for this 2009 report: Lynchburg, Roanoke, Blue Ridge, Appomattox, and Huddleston (Figure 1, Table 1).

Of the five stations four have a Period of Record (POR) sufficiently long for a 30-year normal (1971–2000); however, Huddleston lacks temperature data. The normal for Blue Ridge is based on a POR from 1996–2008. Monthly averages and deviations from normal are presented for all five stations for precipitation, and for all except Huddleston for temperature.

In addition to the summary information available in this report, a near real-time data stream has been made available to the MIDN through a Web interface for the weather observing stations, along with monthly, seasonal, and annual summaries. The Web interface is accessible through the following link: http://climate.met.psu.edu/gmaps/NPS_DEVELOPMENT/interface.php.

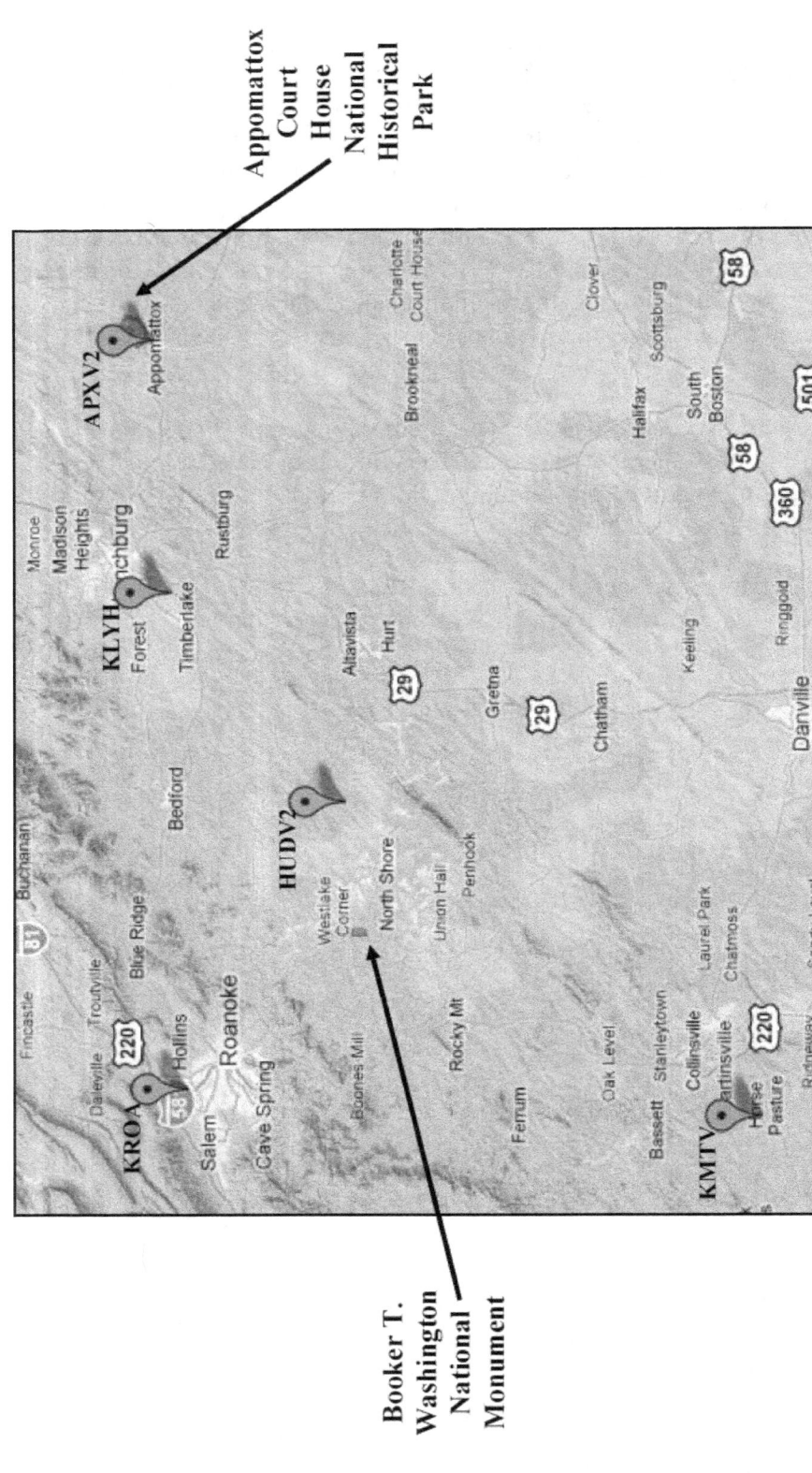

Figure 1. Location of weather observing stations around Appomattox Court House National Historical Park and Booker T. Washington National Monument selected as most representative of the parks in 2009.

Table 1. List of weather observing stations around Appomattox Court House National Historical Park and Booker T. Washington National Monument selected as most representative of the parks in 2009.

Weather Station	Weather Network	Station Name	Period of Record (POR)		Percentage of Time Reporting Temperature for 2009	Percentage of Time Reporting Precipitation for 2009	Percentage of Time Reporting Temperature for entire POR	Percentage of Time Reporting Precipitation for entire POR
KLYH	FAA	Lynchburg	02/01/1948	Present	100.0	100.0	95.8	95.8
KROA	FAA	Roanoke	02/01/1948	Present	100.0	100.0	95.6	95.6
KMTV	FAA	Blue Ridge	01/01/1996	Present	96.7	96.7	93.3	35.4
APXV2	COOP	Appomattox	11/01/1937	Present	96.4	100.0	94.9*	96.0
HUDV2	COOP	Huddleston	01/01/1960	Present	-	100.0	-	99.2

* Percentage of time reporting temperature for Appomattox is based upon a Period of Record beginning on 11/01/1961. The station did not report temperature prior to this date.

Temperature Summary

Temperatures in 2009 were slightly below average for Appomattox Court House NHP and Booker T. Washington NM (Table 2) despite a very mild February and November (Tables 3 and 4). Variability was the main theme, with below-average anomalies in five months while the other seven months featured near to above-average temperatures (Figures 2 and 3)[1].

January was colder than average, with mean temperatures ranging from +0.1 to -2.1°F (0 to -1.2°C) from the long-term values (Tables 3 and 4). The lowest readings of the year occurred at mid-month with values in the low single digits °F (~17°C), slightly lower than the typical annual minimums (Table 2). February was noticeably milder, with mean temperatures varying from 39.1°F (3.9°C) at Appomattox to 42.2°F (5.7°C) at Roanoke (Table 3). Near-normal temperatures ruled in March, leading to a winter which ranked the 37th coolest in 115 years for the Western Piedmont (Table 5). There were also a near-normal number of cold days during the winter (Table 2).

Spring was consistently milder than normal, as all three months noted small positive anomalies at each of the representative weather stations (Table 4). May had the largest positive departures, with Blue Ridge registering 3.1°F (1.7°C) above normal (Table 4). Much of the warmth was due to mild nights (Figure 3). Overall, this season ranked in the normal range for the Western Piedmont (Table 5).

The summer months featured cooler-than-average weather during all of July and much of September. In fact, July had the largest negative anomalies, ranging from -1.7 to -4.2°F (-0.9 to -2.3°C) (Table 4). August brought above-seasonal temperatures (Figure 2) and below-normal temperatures returned in September, specifically to Appomattox and Lynchburg (Table 4). The number of hot days was well below normal. Only nine days reached or exceeded 90°F (32.2°C), compared with normal numbers around 25 days (Table 2). Accordingly, the highest readings of 2009 fell short of the normal values, only topping out at 92°F (33.3°C) compared to 96°F (35.6°C) (Table 2). Summer of 2009 ranked the 15th coolest in the last 115 years (Table 5).

A very mild November was sandwiched between two cool autumn months. October and December were dominated by cooler than average days and nights (Figures 2 and 3). The number of sub-freezing nights was very close to the long term average (Table 2). November's departure from normal varied from +2.4°F (1.3°C) at Blue Ridge to +4.2°F (2.3°C) at Roanoke (Table 4). The autumn ranked as the 32nd coolest in 115 years for the Western Piedmont (Table 5). The length of the growing season was virtually normal when compared to the 1971–2000 average and despite maximum temperatures averaging below normal, minimums were consistently above average (Table 2).

---

[1] The maps in Figures 2 and 3 were created using estimates from the Parameter-elevation Regressions on Independent Slopes Model (PRISM). PRISM uses an interpolation scheme for temperature between actual observations and corrects these estimates for changes in topography across the region (Daly et al. 2002). More information can be found at http://www.prism.oregonstate.edu/.

Table 2. Status of 2009 temperature indicators compared to the 30-year normal (1971–2000) at the Lynchburg (KLYH), Roanoke (KROA) and Appomattox (APXV2) weather observing stations.

Temperature Indicator	Lynchburg 2009	Lynchburg 1971–2000	Roanoke 2009	Roanoke 1971–2000	Appomattox 2009	Appomattox 1971–2000
Average Annual Temperature	55.1°F 12.8°C	55.4°F 13°C	57.3°F 14.1°C	56.3°F 13.5°C	55.2°F 12.9°C	55.7°F 13.2°C
Average Annual Maximum Temperature	65.0°F 18.3°C	66.9°F 19.4°C	66.8°F 19.3°C	67.3°F 19.6°C	66.4°F 19.1°C	67.4°F 19.7°C
Summer Maximum (highest temperature)	91.9°F 33.3°C	95.0°F 35°C	92.0°F 33.3°C	95.8°F 35.4°C	92.0°F 33.3°C	96.1°F 35.6°C
Hot Days (days with Tmax≥90°F/32°C)	9	24	9	27	8	26
Average Annual Minimum Temperature	45.1°F 7.3°C	44.1°F 6.7°C	47.9°F 8.8°C	45.5°F 7.5°C	44.0°F 6.7°C	43.9°F 6.6°C
Winter Minimum (lowest temperature)	1.0°F -17.2°C	4.1°F -15.5°C	3.0°F -16.1°C	4.6°F -15.2°C	2.0°F -16.7°C	3.4°F -15.9°C
Cold Days (days with Tmax≤32°F/0°F)	9	9	6	10	6	8
Sub-freezing Nights (days with Tmin≤32°F/0°C)	90	89	69	87	102	98
Cold Winter Nights (days with Tmin≤0°F/-17.8°C)	0	1	0	1	0	1
Growing Season Length (days between last spring 32°F/0°C and first fall 32°F/0°C)	202	206	211	212	194	198

Table 3. Summary of 2009 monthly average temperatures for selected stations.

Station name	Station	Jan	Feb	Mar	Apr	May	Jun	Jul	Aug	Sep	Oct	Nov	Dec	Annual
Lynchburg	KLYH	32.8°F	39.4°F	45.3°F	55.9°F	64.8°F	72.3°F	72.6°F	75.6°F	66.8°F	55.5°F	49.5°F	34.8°F	55.1°F
		0.4°C	4.1°C	7.4°C	13.3°C	18.2°C	22.4°C	22.6°C	24.2°C	19.3°C	13.1°C	9.7°C	1.6°C	12.8°C
Roanoke	KROA	35.9°F	42.2°F	48.3°F	57.5°F	65.4°F	74.1°F	73.3°F	76.1°F	68.8°F	57.3°F	51.5°F	37.3°F	57.3°F
		2.2°C	5.7°C	9.1°C	14.2°C	18.5°C	23.4°C	22.9°C	24.5°C	20.4°C	14.0°C	10.8°C	2.9°C	14.1°C
Blue Ridge	KMTV	35.3°F	41.8°F	48.0°F	56.6°F	67.0°F	74.9°F	74.7°F	76.3°F	68.4°F	57.1°F	50.6°F	37.3°F	57.9°F
		1.8°C	5.4°C	8.9°C	17.5°C	19.5°C	23.8°C	23.7°C	24.6°C	20.2°C	14.0°C	10.3°C	2.9°C	14.4°C
Appomattox	APXV2	32.1°F	39.1°F	44.3°F	55.4°F	64.0°F	72.1°F	71.7°F	75.3°F	66.4°F	54.6°F	49.0°F	34.9°F	55.2°F
		0.1°C	3.9°C	6.8°C	13.0°C	17.8°C	22.3°C	22.1°C	24.1°C	19.1°C	12.5°C	9.4°C	1.6°C	12.9°C

Table 4. Summary of 2009 departure from normal temperature based on 30-year normal (1971–2000) for selected stations.

Station name	Station	Jan	Feb	Mar	Apr	May	Jun	Jul	Aug	Sep	Oct	Nov	Dec	Annual
Lynchburg	KLYH	-1.7°F	1.6°F	-0.7°F	0.6°F	1.4°F	1.3°F	-2.5°F	1.8°F	-0.3°F	-0.6°F	2.9°F	-3.4°F	-0.3°F
		-0.9°C	0.9°C	-0.4°C	0.3°C	0.8°C	0.7°C	-1.4°C	1.0°C	-0.2°C	-0.3°C	1.6°C	-1.9°C	-0.2°C
Roanoke	KROA	0.1°F	3.1°F	1.1°F	1.4°F	1.3°F	2.2°F	-2.9°F	1.4°F	1.1°F	0.6°F	4.2°F	-1.8°F	1.0°F
		0.1°C	1.7°C	0.6°C	0.8°C	0.7°C	1.2°C	-1.6°C	0.8°C	0.6°C	0.4°C	2.3°C	-1.0°C	0.5°C
Blue Ridge	KMTV	-0.7°F	3.3°F	1.6°F	1.5°F	3.1°F	2.8°F	-1.7°F	1.3°F	0.1°F	-0.2°F	2.4°F	-1.9°F	1.0°F
		-0.4°C	1.8°C	0.9°C	0.8°C	1.7°C	1.6°C	-0.9°C	0.7°C	0.1°C	-0.1°C	1.3°C	-1.1°C	0.5°C
Appomattox	APXV2	-2.1°F	1.7°F	-1.1°F	0.5°F	0.7°F	0.5°F	-4.2°F	1.0°F	-1.3°F	-1.4°F	2.4°F	-3.1°F	-0.5°F
		-1.2°C	0.9°C	-0.6°C	0.3°C	0.4°C	0.3°C	-2.3°C	0.6°C	-0.7°C	-0.8°C	1.3°C	-1.7°C	-0.3°C

Table 5. Seasonal temperature and precipitation rankings over 115 years for the Western Piedmont (NOAA 2010).

Climate Division 3 Rankings Western Piedmont	Jan–Feb–Mar WINTER	Apr–May–Jun SPRING	Jul–Aug–Sep SUMMER	Oct–Nov–Dec AUTUMN
Temperature-2009	78	71	100	83
Precipitation-2009	89	17	84	2

1 = warmest/wettest year and 115 = coldest/driest year

Appomattox Court House National Historical Park and Booker T. Washington National Monument Departure from Average Monthly Maximum Temperature 2009 vs. 1971–2000

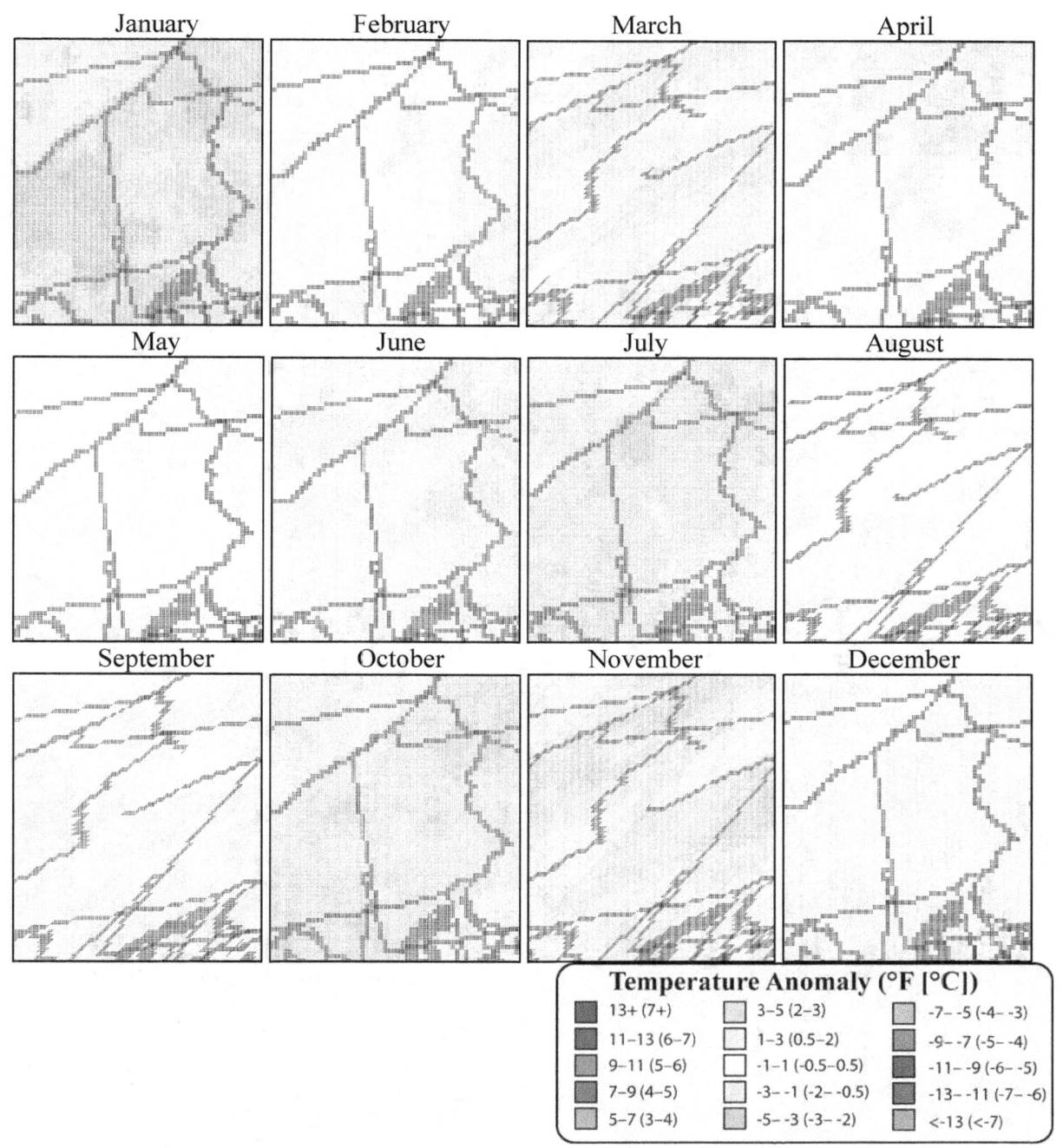

Figure 2. Maps showing departure from average monthly maximum temperature compared to the 30-year normal (1971–2000).

Appomattox Court House National Historical Park
and Booker T. Washington National Monument
Departure from Average Monthly Minimum Temperature
2009 vs. 1971–2000

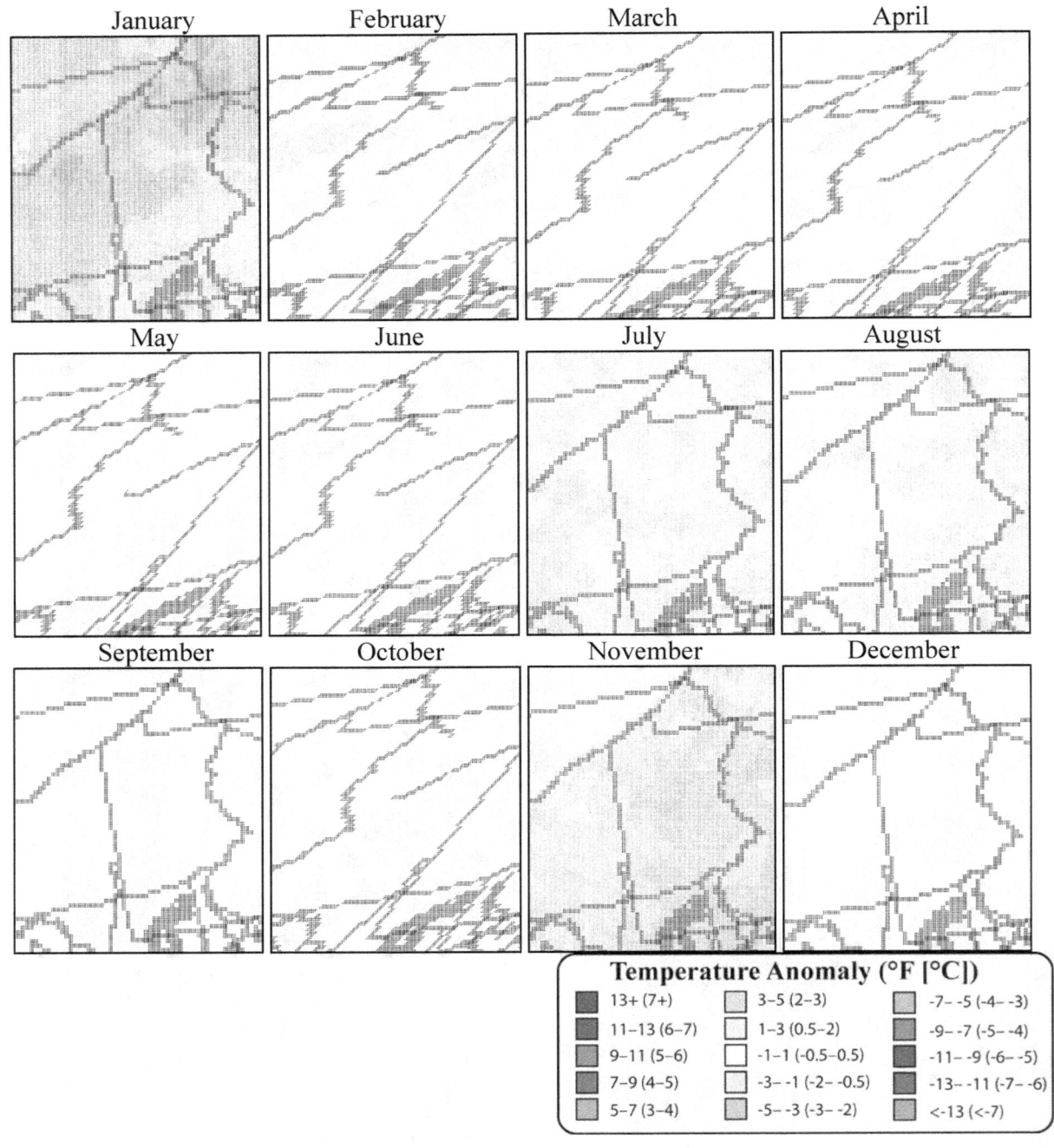

Figure 3. Maps showing departure from average monthly minimum temperature compared to the 30-year normal (1971–2000).

Precipitation Summary

The year began with a dry spell which continued through April at Appomattox Court House NHP and Booker T. Washington NM. Oddly, the seasons alternated with a dry winter, wet spring, dry summer, and one of the wettest autumns on record (Table 5). Annual precipitation ranged from 3.6 in (91 mm), or about an average month of rain and snow at Lynchburg, to 11.3 in (287 mm), or about three extra months of precipitation at Roanoke (Table 6). As expected, the number of heavy rain days also exceeded the long-term average (Table 6).

January started with heavy precipitation, a total of 2.1 in (53 mm) falling on the 7th (Table 7). However the rest of the month was rather dry followed by February which proved to be the driest month of 2009 (Figure 4). Precipitation in February was measured at 9–45 percent of normal (Tables 8 and 9). March brought closer to average rain and snowfall, as 2.6 in (66 mm) was tallied at Blue Ridge and 4.5 in (114 mm) was measured at Appomattox (Table 8). Three long dry spells marked this season. The periods from January 12–27, February 13–28, and March 3–13 had no measurable precipitation across the region (Table 7). Overall, the winter months (January, February and March) were the 26th driest since 1895 (Table 5).

The spring months of May and June were significantly wetter, aided by an anomalously damp May, with 7.0 in (179 mm) in Lynchburg, 171 percent of normal precipitation for the month (Tables 8 and 9). Very heavy rain, totaling 2.2 in (56 mm), occurred on May 14, though it was preceded by a long dry spell from April 22–May 3 (Table 7). Overall, the spring in the Western Piedmont ranked as the 17th wettest in 115 years of records (Table 5).

Summer rainfall was highly varied across the region, as evidenced by the range of precipitation during July. This month brought a pittance, with 1.4 in (37 mm) at Blue Ridge and an overabundance of 5.8 in (149 mm) at Roanoke (Table 8). Since there were no effects from tropical storms during the summer of 2009, overall, this season averaged on the dry side, ranked as the 31st driest in 115 years for the Western Piedmont (Table 5). Two notably wet days occurred with 2.5 in (64 mm) on August 23 and 2.2 in (56 mm) falling on September 26 (Table 7).

The last quarter of the year was very wet. October, though, was rather dry, with all representative weather stations tallying less than 95 percent of the normal rainfall (Table 9). In contrast, November and December had well over 200 percent of normal precipitation at the majority of weather stations (Table 9). The autumn precipitation total was more than double the 1971–2000 normal amount, and the wettest day of 2009 occurred on November 12, when 2.9 in (74 mm) fell (Tables 6 and 7). Snowfall was well above normal, with most sections measuring more than 20 in (51 cm), compared with long-term averages of less than 12 in (30 cm) (Table 6). Much of the snow for 2009 fell in December.

Appomattox Court House National Historical Park
and Booker T. Washington National Monument
Percent of Average Monthly Precipitation
2009 vs. 1971–2000

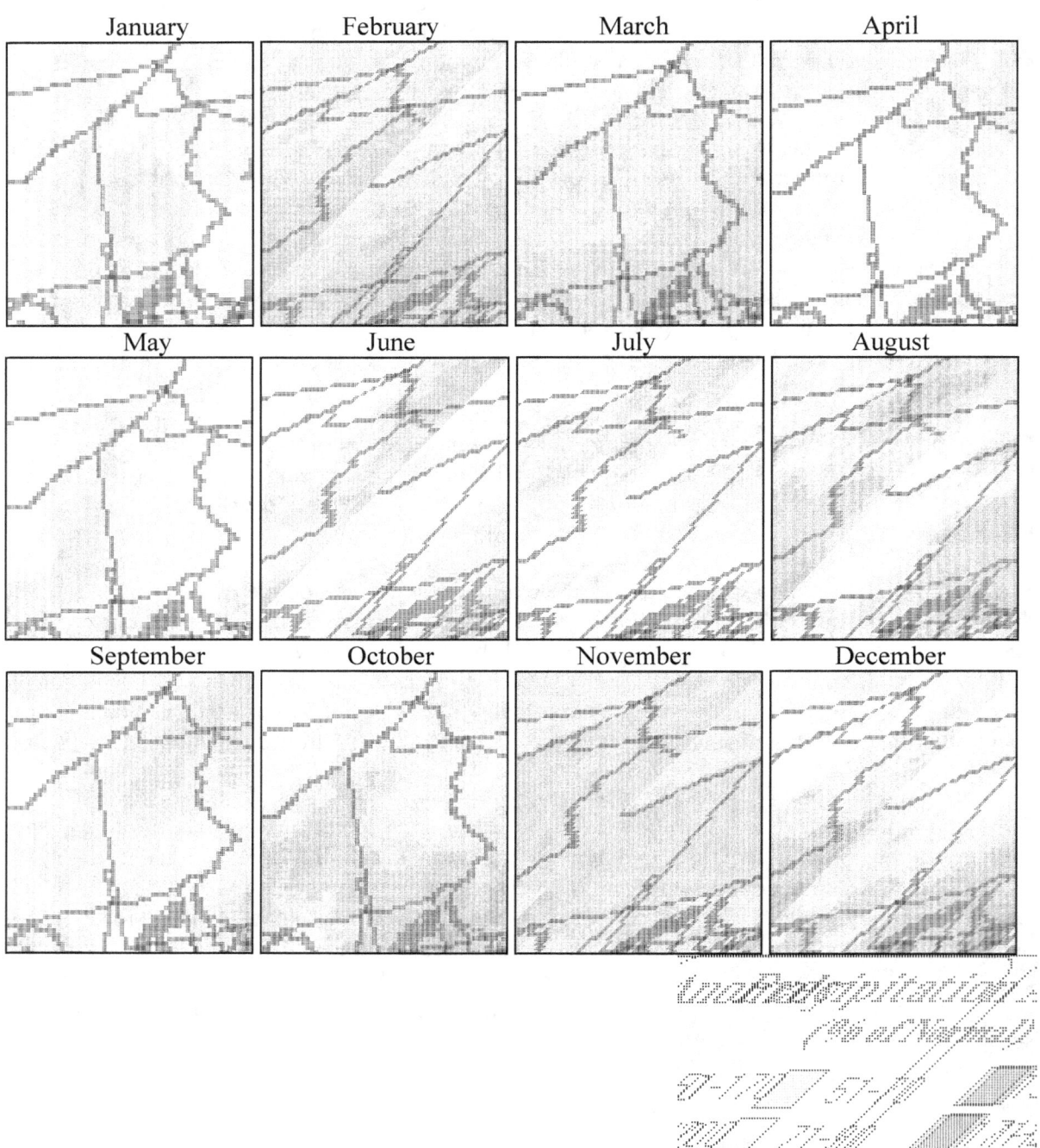

Figure 4. Maps showing percent of average monthly precipitation compared to the 30-year normal (1971–2000).

Table 6. Status of 2009 precipitation indicators compared to the 30-year normal (1971–2000) at the Lynchburg (KLYH), Roanoke (KROA), Appomattox (APXV2) and Huddleston (HUDV2) weather observing stations.

Precipitation Indicator	Lynchburg 2009	Lynchburg 1971–2000	Roanoke 2009	Roanoke 1971–2000	Appomattox 2009	Appomattox 1971–2000	Huddleston 2009	Huddleston 1971–2000
Annual Precipitation	46.9 in 1,191 mm	43.3 in 1,099 mm	53.8 in 1,367 mm	42.5 in 1,080 mm	54.4 in 1,382 mm	45.9 in 1,166 mm	52.4 in 1,331 mm	42.9 in 1,090 mm
Autumn (Oct, Nov, Dec) Precipitation	18.2 in 462 mm	9.8 in 249 mm	18.4 in 467 mm	9.2 in 234 mm	20.6 in 523 mm	10.5 in 267 mm	18.4 in 467 mm	9.9 in 252 mm
Heavy Rain (days with ≥1.0 in (25 mm) rain)	12	11	16	10	17	12	14	12
Extreme Rain (days with ≥2.0 in (51 mm) rain)	2	1	3	3	3	3	3	3
Micro-drought (strings of 7+ days without rain)	13	8	10	9	12	12	10	12
Annual Snowfall	23.7 in 60.2 cm	11.0 in 27.9 cm	23 in 58.4 cm	10.9 in 27.7 cm	19.1 in 48.5 cm	13.3 in 33.8 cm	27.0 in 68.6 cm	11.2 in 28.4 cm
Snow (days with ≥0.1 in (0.3 cm) snow)	8	7	7	7	4	5	4	3
Moderate Snow (days with ≥2.0 in (5.0 cm) snow)	4	2	3	2	3	3	2	1
Heavy Snow (days with ≥5.0 in (12.7 cm) snow)	2	0.4	2	1	2	1	2	0.1

Table 7. Top five wettest days and top five dry spells (consecutive days with a trace or less of rainfall) during 2009 from weather observing stations at Lynchburg (KLYH), Roanoke (KROA), Blue Ridge (KMTV), Appomattox (APXV2) and Huddleston (HUDV2).

Wettest Days in 2009	Dry Spells in 2009
Nov. 12: 2.9 in (74 mm)	Jun. 18–Jul. 4
Aug. 23: 2.5 in (64 mm)	Jan. 12–27
Sept. 26: 2.2 in (56 mm)	Feb. 13–28
May 14: 2.2 in (56 mm)	Apr. 22–May 3
Jan. 7: 2.1 in (53 mm)	Mar. 3–13

13

Table 8. Summary of 2009 monthly total precipitation for selected stations.

Station name	Station	Jan	Feb	Mar	Apr	May	Jun	Jul	Aug	Sep	Oct	Nov	Dec	Annual
Lynchburg	KLYH	3.1 in	1.1 in	3.2 in	2.9 in	7.0 in	3.7 in	3.1 in	2.4 in	2.2 in	3.2 in	8.2 in	6.8 in	46.9 in
		80 mm	29 mm	82 mm	73 mm	179 mm	94 mm	79 mm	60 mm	55 mm	81 mm	208 mm	173 mm	1,193 mm
Roanoke	KROA	2.7 in	1.2 in	3.5 in	3.2 in	6.9 in	4.5 in	5.8 in	4.4 in	3.1 in	2.7 in	7.4 in	8.2 in	53.8 in
		69 mm	31 mm	88 mm	81 mm	175 mm	115 mm	149 mm	113 mm	80 mm	69 mm	189 mm	209 mm	1,367 mm
Blue Ridge	KMTV	3.2 in	1.5 in	2.6 in	2.8 in	3.6 in	3.4 in	1.4 in	4.2 in	2.3 in	2.8 in	7.6 in	5.6 in	41.0 in
		82 mm	38 mm	66 mm	71 mm	91 mm	86 mm	37 mm	105 mm	57 mm	70 mm	193 mm	143 mm	1,041 mm
Appomattox	APXV2	3.4 in	0.3 in	4.5 in	3.6 in	5.8 in	5.4 in	4.1 in	4.1 in	2.6 in	2.8 in	9.5 in	8.3 in	54.4 in
		87 mm	8 mm	113 mm	90 mm	148 mm	138 mm	104 mm	104 mm	67 mm	72 mm	240 mm	211 mm	1,381 mm
Huddleston	HUDV2	3.9 in	0.8 in	4.3 in	2.9 in	5.3 in	5.7 in	3.7 in	4.0 in	3.3 in	2.9 in	8.5 in	7.1 in	52.4 in
		98 mm	21 mm	110 mm	74 mm	136 mm	146 mm	93 mm	101 mm	83 mm	74 mm	215 mm	179 mm	1,330 mm

Table 9. Summary of 2009 percent of normal precipitation based on 30-year normal (1971–2000) for selected stations.

Station name	Station	Jan	Feb	Mar	Apr	May	Jun	Jul	Aug	Sep	Oct	Nov	Dec	Annual
Lynchburg	KLYH	89	37	84	83	171	98	71	70	56	94	258	211	108
Roanoke	KROA	84	40	91	89	163	122	145	118	81	86	231	287	127
Blue Ridge	KMTV	85	45	58	75	83	86	33	119	53	80	250	173	95
Appomattox	APXV2	95	9	106	99	129	153	92	108	59	73	262	271	121
Huddleston	HUDV2	104	27	108	82	134	170	98	123	77	84	253	230	124

14

Drought Status

There are a number of drought indices used to estimate the severity of drought in an area using algorithms that incorporate recent temperatures, rainfall, soil moisture, and other information (http://www.drought.gov). The main indices we report are the Palmer Drought Severity Index (PDSI) and the United States Drought Monitor (DM) – Drought Intensity Index. While both indices provide excellent summary information on broad-scale conditions, local conditions (such as at the park scale) may vary.

The PDSI is a soil moisture algorithm calibrated for relatively homogeneous regions and is calculated on a monthly basis using precipitation and temperature data, as well as the water content of the soil. The values vary between extremely moist (>4.0) and extreme drought (<-4.0) with "normal" values ranging between -1.9 and 1.9. The long-term average is "zero". Monthly PDSI values for the Western Piedmont in 2009 are shown in Figure 5.

The DM – Drought Intensity Index is a synthesis of multiple indices (including the PDSI) and impacts, which represents a consensus of federal and academic scientists (NIDIS 2010). The DM produces a summary map of drought intensity for the nation and all states each week. It is on a scale ranging from abnormally dry (D0) to exceptional drought (D4). Mid-month (i.e., the second or third week) values for Virginia (Figure 6) and the Southeast (Figure 7) are shown for 2009.

According to the PDSI, 2009 started with normal conditions, with drier conditions intensifying during February, and then approaching zero as spring began (Figure 5). It was not until May when 29 consecutive months with below-zero values of the PDSI finally ended. However, the moist weather was short-lived, as a dry summer brought back drier conditions. A record wet late fall finally extinguished the dry conditions. Compared with the previous two years, 2009 had much more favorable conditions. The PDSI value was only below -1 for two months, unlike every month in 2008.

The DM – Drought Severity Index for Virginia (Figure 6) and the Southeast (Figure 7) shows a pattern similar to the PDSI for the growing season (May through October); abnormally dry (D0) from July to October.

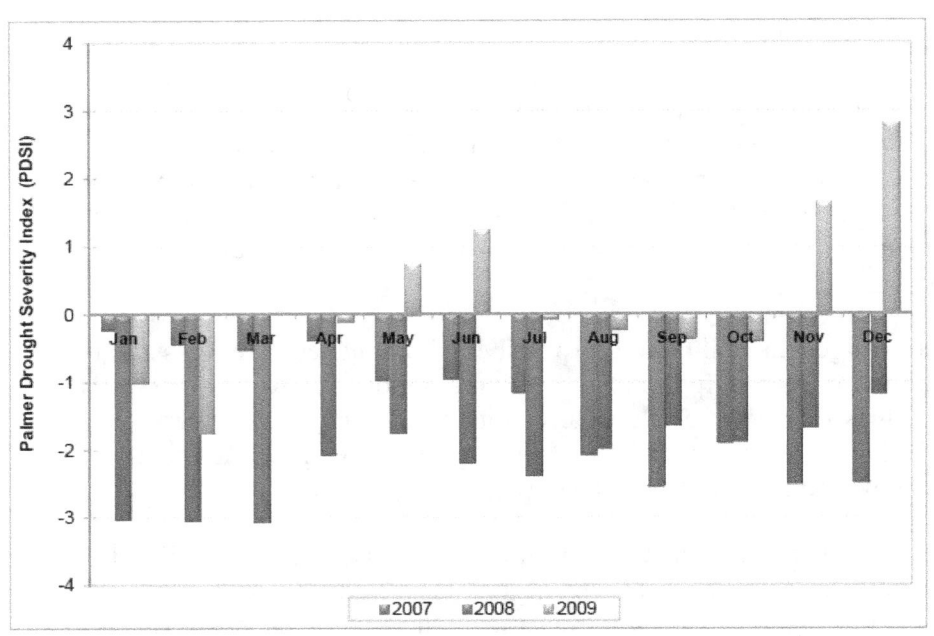

Figure 5. Palmer Drought Severity Index (PDSI) for the Western Piedmont, 2007–2009.

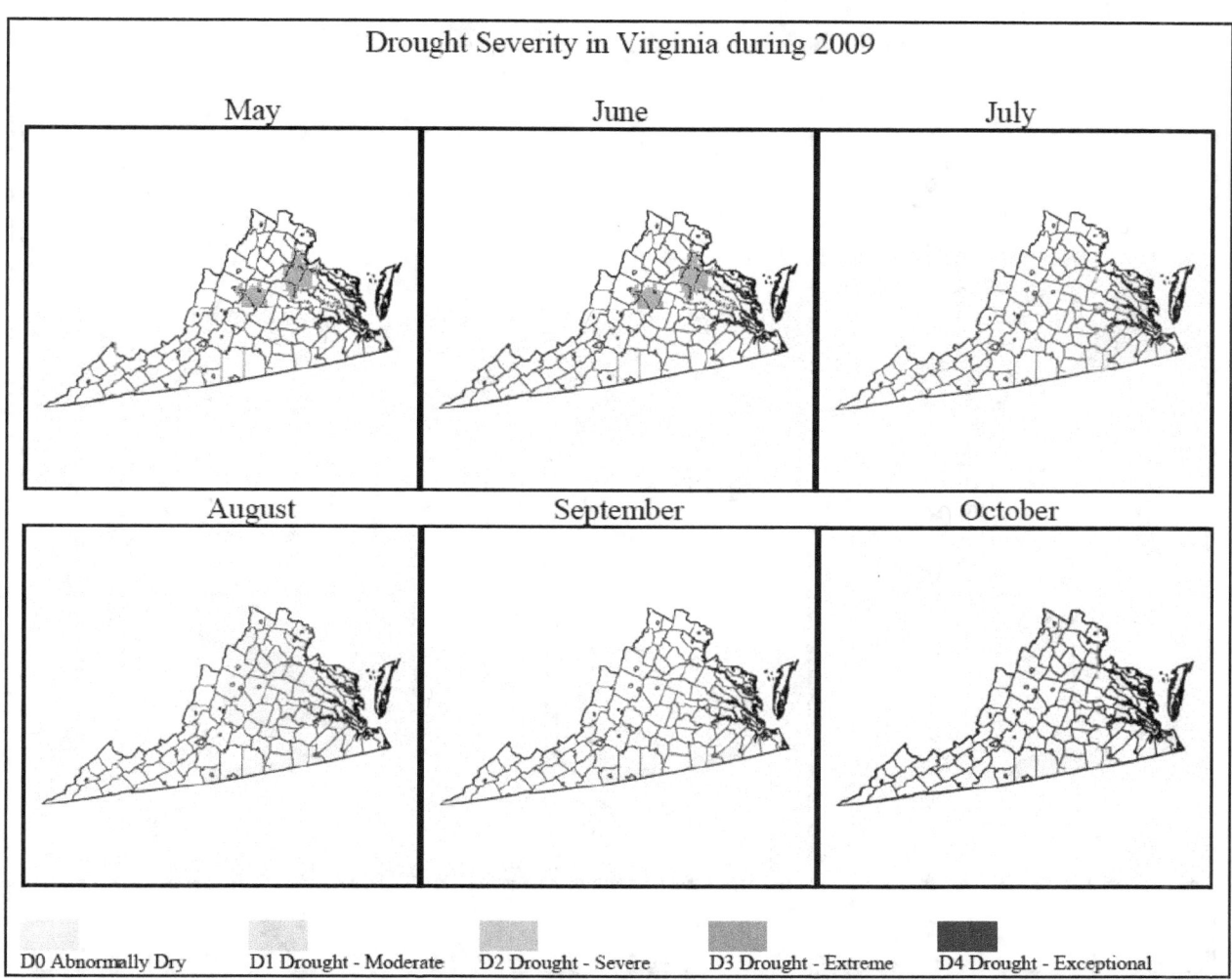

Figure 6. Mid-month values of the Palmer Drought Severity Index for Virginia in 2009.

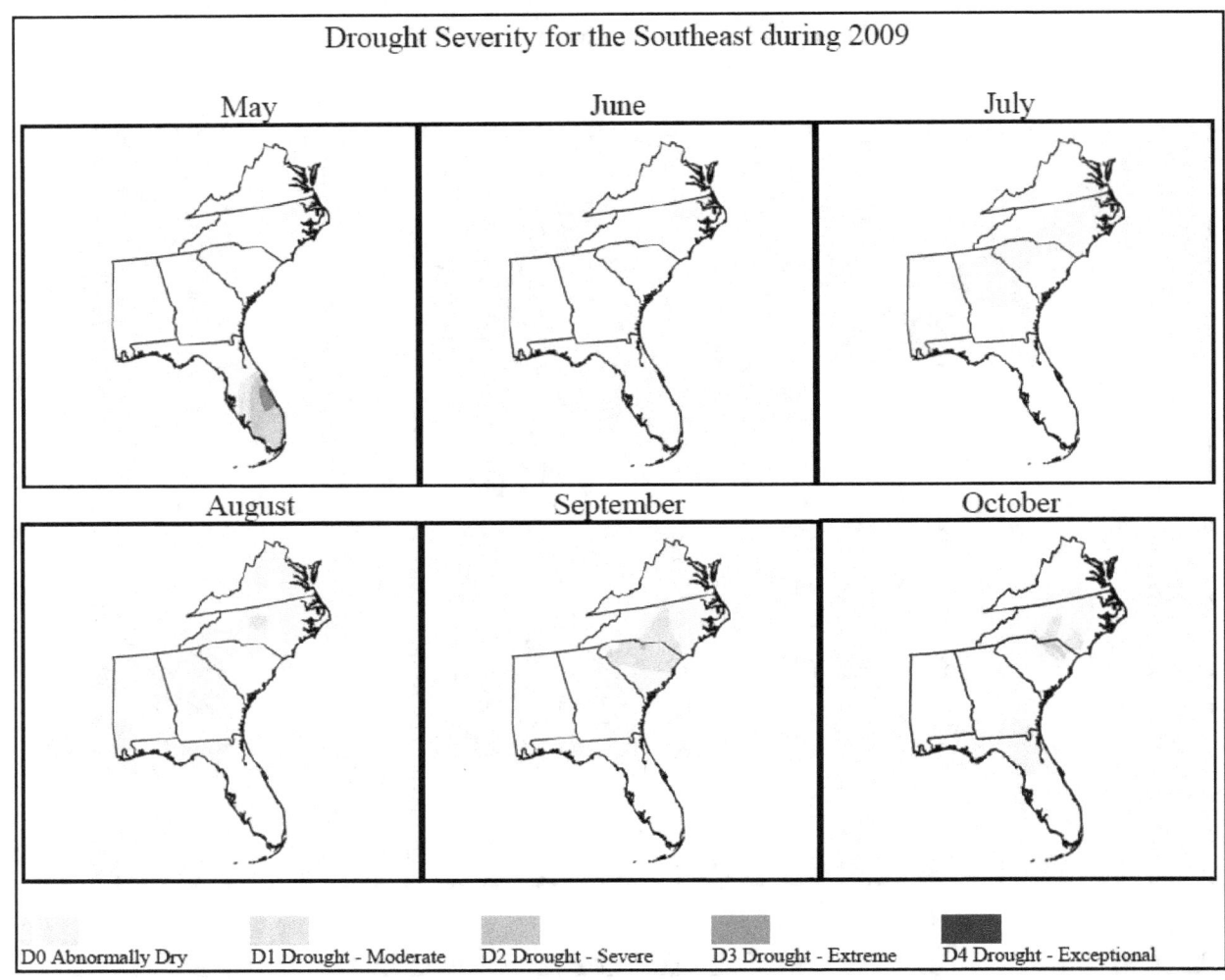

Figure 7. Mid-month values of the Palmer Drought Severity Index for the Southeast in 2009.

References

Bureau of Land Management. 1997. Remote Automatic Weather Station (RAWS) and Remote Environmental Monitoring Systems (REMS) standards. RAWS/REMS Support Facility. Boise, ID.

Comiskey, J. A., and K. K. Callahan. 2008. Mid-Atlantic Network vital signs monitoring plan. Natural Resource Report NPS/MIDN/NRR—2008/071. National Park Service, Fort Collins, CO.

Daly, C., W. P. Gibson, G. H. Taylor, G. L. Johnson, and P. Pasteris. 2002. A knowledge-based approach to the statistical mapping of climate. Climate Research 22:99–113.

Davey, C. A., K. T. Redmond, and D. B. Simeral. 2006. Weather and Climate Inventory, National Park Service, Mid-Atlantic Network. Natural Resource Technical Report NPS/MIDN/NRTR—2006/013. National Park Service, Fort Collins, Colorado.

Gawtry, S., and J. Stenger. 2007. Climate Summary, Shenandoah National Park. Natural Resources Report NPS/NER/NRR—2007/017. National Park Service, Philadelphia, PA

Knight, P., T. Wisniewski, C. Bahrmann, and S. Miller. In preparation. Weather and Climate Monitoring Protocol for the Eastern Rivers and Mountains Network and the Mid-Atlantic Network. Natural Resource Technical Report NPS/MIDN/NRTR—2010/XXX. National Park Service, Fort Collins, CO.

Kocin, P. J., and L. W. Uccellini. 2004. Northeast Snowstorms Volume 1: Overview. Meteorological Monographs. Vol 32. No 54. American Meteorological Society. Boston, MA.

National Assessment Synthesis Team. 2001. Climate Change Impacts on United States: The Potential Consequences of Climate Variability and Change. Report for the U.S. Global Change Research Program. Cambridge University Press, Cambridge, UK.

National Oceanic and Atmospheric Administration (NOAA). 2010. National Climatic Data Center. Climate of 2009 – Annual Review, Global and U.S. Summary. http://lwf.ncdc.noaa.gov/oa/climate/research/2009/ann/us-summary.html.

National Integrated Drought Information System (NIDIS). 2010. National Climate Data Center and United States Department of Agriculture. http://drought.unl.edu/dm/archive.html.

NPS 340/105690, 404/105690, September 2010

www.ingramcontent.com/pod-product-compliance
Lightning Source LLC
Chambersburg PA
CBHW080943290526
45795CB00007BA/2874